P9-AQH-684

The Lincoln-Douglas Debates

by Michael Burgan

Content Adviser: Roger D. Bridges, Ph.D.,
President,
The Abraham Lincoln Association

Reading Adviser: Rosemary G. Palmer, Ph.D.,
Department of Literacy, College of Education,
Boise State University

COMPASS POINT BOOKS
MINNEAPOLIS, MINNESOTA

Compass Point Books
3109 West 50th Street, #115
Minneapolis, MN 55410

Visit Compass Point Books on the Internet at *www.compasspointbooks.com*
or e-mail your request to *custserv@compasspointbooks.com*

On the cover: Abraham Lincoln and Stephen Douglas at a debate

Photographs ©: Bettmann/Corbis, cover, 4, 37; Prints Old & Rare, back cover (far left); Library
of Congress, back cover, 9, 10, 16, 23, 39, 40, 41; The Granger Collection, New York, 6, 8,
15, 17, 18, 20, 24; North Wind Picture Archives, 12; MPI/Getty Images, 19; Abraham Lincoln
Historical Digitization Project, Northern Illinois University Libraries, 21; Corbis, 26, 28, 31;
Kean Collection/Getty Images, 30; Joseph Sohm/Corbis, 33; Courtesy Lockport Street Gallery,
Plainfield, Illinois/art by Paul Ashack, 34.

Editor: Julie Gassman
Page Production: The Design Lab
Photo Researcher: Svetlana Zhurkin
Cartographer: XNR Productions, Inc.
Library Consultant: Kathleen Baxter

Creative Director: Keith Griffin
Editorial Director: Carol Jones
Managing Editor: Catherine Neitge

Library of Congress Cataloging-in-Publication Data
Burgan, Michael.
  The Lincoln-Douglas debates / by Michael Burgan.
     p. cm.—(We the people)
  Includes bibliographical references and index.
  ISBN 0-7565-1632-3 (hard cover)
  ISBN 0-7565-1767-2 (paperback)
  1. Lincoln-Douglas debates, 1858—Juvenile literature. 2. Lincoln, Abraham, 1809–1865—
Juvenile literature. 3. Douglas, Stephen Arnold, 1813–1861—Juvenile literature. I. Title. II.
Series: We the people (Series) (Compass Point Books)
E457.4.B89 2006
326'.0973—dc22   2005025084

TABLE OF CONTENTS

DEBATING SLAVERY

On a hot August day in 1858, thousands of people poured into the Illinois town of Ottawa. They braved the heat to hear a debate between Stephen Douglas and Abraham Lincoln. The two men were candidates for the U.S. Senate.

Stephen Douglas stands behind Abraham Lincoln as he addresses a crowd during one of their famous debates.

4

The Senate, along with the U.S. House of Representatives, makes laws for the country.

Douglas belonged to the Democratic Party, one of the two major political groups in the nation. He had served as one of Illinois' two U.S. senators since 1847. Lincoln, who was a member of the Republican Party, had once served in the House of Representatives. Now he wanted to take Douglas' spot in the Senate.

Douglas was known as the "Little Giant." Just 5 feet 4 inches (162 centimeters) tall, he was one of the most important members of the Democratic Party. Lincoln, who was a foot taller, challenged Douglas to a series of debates before the November election. Douglas agreed to meet Lincoln seven times. Each man hoped to convince the voters that he was the best person to represent Illinois in the Senate.

In the debates, Lincoln and Douglas offered their opinions and questioned each other on various issues. The most important issue of the day was slavery. During the 1850s, many Americans held opposing views on slavery.

Nineteen-year-old Lincoln, second from left, watches a slave auction with disgust.

Northern states had either already outlawed slavery or never allowed it at all. Many people in the North did not want slavery to spread to new U.S. territories or states. A smaller number of Northerners called abolitionists wanted slavery to end everywhere in the country as soon as possible.

Southerners, for the most part, accepted slavery. Southern states relied on slaves to care for the crops that were grown there and sold around the world. Some slaves also had trained skills, such as carpentry or shipbuilding. Most Southerners feared their economy would collapse if slavery ended. They thought the government should protect slavery and allow it to expand into new territories.

Douglas and his supporters in Illinois thought the citizens of each new state or territory had the right to decide if they wanted slavery. This idea was called popular sovereignty. Lincoln and the Republicans rejected popular sovereignty. They did not want slavery to expand into other parts of the country. Lincoln believed that slavery in general was wrong, but he was not an abolitionist. He hoped slavery would slowly end where it already existed. The two men's difference in views was at the center of the debates.

Even though it was a state campaign, the whole country followed the debates. Lincoln became popular with Republicans all over the United States. Thanks in part to the fame Lincoln won from the debates, he was chosen as the Republican candidate for president in 1860. In that

The 1860 Republican convention nominated Abraham Lincoln as a presidential candidate.

election, he defeated Douglas and two other candidates. In 1860, slavery was still the main issue dividing the nation. And slavery would soon lead to the Civil War. After the election, some Southern slave states seceded to make sure they could keep slavery. Lincoln led the North as it fought to keep the country united and eventually end slavery.

NEWCOMERS TO ILLINOIS

Abraham Lincoln and Stephen Douglas had several things in common. Although both men made their political careers in Illinois, neither was born in the state. Lincoln was born in Kentucky in 1809. His family farmed there before moving to Indiana. As a boy, Lincoln did not regularly attend school, but he learned to read and deeply loved books. In 1830, his family settled in Illinois.

Lincoln left his family's farm at the age of 21. The following year, he moved to New Salem, Illinois. He served in the local militia during the Black Hawk War, a war between American settlers

Abraham Lincoln

9

and Indians. After the war, he returned to New Salem to live and work. He won his first political campaign in 1834, when he was elected to the state legislature, called the Illinois General Assembly. At that time, Lincoln belonged to the Whig Party. This party promoted industry and banking in the United States. While in the legislature, Lincoln studied to become a lawyer.

Stephen Douglas

Douglas was born in 1813 in Vermont. Like Lincoln, he grew up on a farm. But unlike his opponent, Douglas spent three months every year at a local school. Later, he attended an academy in New York. The school was similar to a college.

Douglas moved to Illinois in 1833 and studied law. Like

10

Lincoln, he became a lawyer and entered local politics. In 1835, Illinois lawmakers elected Douglas an attorney for the state. The next year, he was elected to the state legislature. As a Democrat, Douglas backed his party's efforts to help farmers and workers move and settle in Western parts of the United States. Douglas also supported building new railroads and canals to move people and goods.

Douglas and Lincoln met each other for the first time as members of the legislature. At times, they shared the same views, even though they belonged to opposing parties. But already they had different views on slavery. In 1837, Douglas voted for an anti-abolition resolution, a statement that expresses an opinion on a political issue. The resolution criticized the goals of U.S. abolitionists and stated that slavery was legal under the U.S. Constitution. Lincoln was one of only six Illinois lawmakers who voted against the resolution. But he supported another resolution that said the U.S. government "has no power, under the constitution to interfere with … slavery in the different States."

The Illinois State House where the Illinois Legislature met

Lincoln served in the Illinois Legislature for eight years. During that time, Douglas left the state legislature and held several jobs related to government and politics. For a time, he served on Illinois' most important court, the state Supreme Court. In 1842, Douglas was elected to the U.S. House of Representatives. He was still in the House in 1847, when Lincoln was elected a representative. The two men, however, did not serve in the House at the same time. By the time Lincoln began his term, Douglas was serving as a U.S. senator. When Lincoln's two-year term ended, he did not run for the House again. He had told voters that he only intended to serve for one term during his 1847 campaign.

SLAVERY IN THE WEST

Lincoln returned to Illinois to practice law. Meanwhile, Douglas became known across the nation for his work in the Senate. One of his goals was for the United States to acquire new lands in the West. Some Whigs opposed adding new territory because slave owners wanted to bring their slaves to these lands. Northern Whigs did not want slavery to spread beyond the South.

While some Whigs simply thought slavery was wrong, others wanted to limit its growth for political reasons. As the United States expanded, Northern states lost some of their influence to the Southern and Western states. If slavery were allowed to spread, the South and West would have more representatives in Congress than the North. The slave states could then control Congress, and the North might never have a chance to limit or end slavery. Slave states could also establish government policies that favored farming, their main source of income.

Those policies might hurt the interests of free states that relied more on trade and manufacturing.

Douglas and other Northern Democrats in Congress wanted the support of Southern slave owners. One way to win that support was by allowing slavery to spread. In 1848, Douglas began to speak in support of popular sovereignty. At the time, Congress was debating whether to allow California to become a state. Lawmakers were also considering whether New Mexico and other Western lands should become U.S. territories. Lawmakers disagreed on whether slavery should be allowed in these areas. Douglas believed that "the control of … [slavery] belongs entirely with the State or Territory … the [U.S.] government cannot touch the subject."

The spread of slavery was threatening to divide the nation. In both the North and South, people spoke about disunion—splitting the United States into two countries. One would allow slavery, and the other would not. Douglas opposed disunion. He hoped to keep the country whole while preserving slavery. One way to do this was to compromise on certain issues.

In the Compromise of 1850, Congress decided to let California enter the Union as a free state. Utah and New Mexico would become U.S. territories, and their residents would decide whether they wanted slavery. Since neither territory had slavery at that time, most people assumed

An 1850 political cartoon shows one senator pulling a gun on another in an argument over California entering the Union as a free state.

15

Kentucky Senator Henry Clay urged the U.S. Senate to adopt the Compromise of 1850 to prevent a civil war.

they would remain free, which satisfied Northerners. Southerners, meanwhile, were glad Congress was supporting popular sovereignty.

16

ARGUMENTS OVER KANSAS

Douglas considered the Compromise of 1850 the "final settlement" of the slavery issue. He urged Americans to "stop the debate, and drop the subject." Slavery, however, remained a problem. Douglas added fuel to the debate in 1854 when he wrote the Kansas-Nebraska Act. This law created the two territories of Kansas and Nebraska. The territories were part of the Louisiana Purchase—lands that the United States had bought from France in 1803.

Under Douglas' act, residents in Kansas and Nebraska could decide for themselves if they wanted slavery.

Some Northerners felt the act had a major problem. It did not follow the

An 1855 poster advertised a meeting to discuss the slavery issue in Kansas.

17

Kansas and Nebraska territories were well above the Missouri Compromise line.

Missouri Compromise of 1820, a series of laws that limited slavery in parts of the Louisiana Purchase. The compromise said slavery would not be allowed in lands north of the line of latitude that formed the southern border of Missouri. Because both Kansas and Nebraska were north of that line, slavery should not have been allowed in these territories. Southern senators, with Douglas' support, repealed the part of the Missouri Compromise that limited the spread of slavery to give the residents in Kansas and Nebraska popular sovereignty.

Most Americans assumed Nebraska would not allow

slavery. It bordered free states and did not have many settlers. But Kansas bordered the slave state of Missouri, and Missouri slave owners wanted slavery in Kansas as well. Soon settlers from Missouri and the South came to Kansas with their slaves. Meanwhile, New Englanders who opposed slavery also came to the territory. Fighting broke out between the people who supported slavery and those who opposed it. By 1856, the territory was known as "Bleeding Kansas."

Five antislavery settlers were killed in Kansas by a pro-slavery group from Missouri in May 1858.

19

ILLINOIS POLITICS

The Kansas-Nebraska Act had a strong impact on politics. Some Northern Democrats believed they could no longer support their party because it had rejected the Missouri Compromise. They joined some Whigs and members of smaller antislavery parties to create the Republican Party.

The first Republican convention was held in Jackson, Michigan, on July 6, 1854.

During the country's elections in 1854, Douglas toured Illinois and gave speeches to help build support for Democratic candidates. He also promoted the Kansas-Nebraska Act. Meanwhile, Abraham Lincoln was running for the Illinois Legislature. He remained a Whig, but he joined in the Republicans' criticism of the Kansas-Nebraska Act.

In October, Lincoln challenged Douglas to let him speak on the same stage as the senator. Douglas declined. So after Douglas gave his speech, Lincoln told the crowd that he would address Douglas' ideas in his own speech the next day. He invited Douglas to attend.

The next afternoon, Lincoln spoke for almost

Lincoln spoke against the Kansas-Nebraska Act in a speech in Peoria, Illinois, in October 1854.

21

three hours. Douglas spoke for almost two hours after Lincoln finished. Two weeks later, the two men again appeared on the same stage. Lincoln made a similar speech both times, saying, "I am … arguing against the extension of a bad thing [slavery], which where it already exists, we must of necessity, manage as best we can." While Lincoln wanted to limit the growth of slavery, he did not wish to abolish it. Both Whigs and Republicans praised Lincoln's speech.

On Election Day, Douglas watched painfully as the Democrats did poorly in Illinois and around the country. In the North and Midwest, many voters chose candidates who opposed the Kansas-Nebraska Act. Lincoln easily won his seat in the legislature, but he decided not to accept it. He wanted to be eligible to be a candidate for the U.S. Senate seat that opened that year.

In the 19th century, voters did not directly elect senators. Instead, state lawmakers chose the senators for their state. Lincoln ran for the Senate as a Whig.

He told Illinois lawmakers
that although he was not an
abolitionist, he opposed
the spread of slavery and
thought it was a moral
evil. Almost half of
those lawmakers were
Democrats who strongly
supported Douglas' views.
Lincoln saw that he could
not win, so he dropped out

Lyman Trumbull

of the race and gave his support to Lyman Trumbull, a
Democrat who opposed slavery and the Kansas-Nebraska
Act. Trumbull won the final vote.

Lincoln was disappointed with his own loss. He told
a friend he might never run for another political office. But
in 1858, he changed his mind. By this time, the Whig Party
had fallen apart and Lincoln had joined the Republican
Party. Slavery was still dividing the nation. The U.S.

23

Dred Scott

Supreme Court had recently made a major decision. In the Dred Scott case of 1857, the nation's most powerful court ruled that slaves, as well as free African-Americans, were not U.S. citizens and, therefore, did not have legal rights. The court also said that slaves could be brought into any territory, even if local laws did not allow slavery.

The Dred Scott decision and the Kansas-Nebraska Act angered Lincoln. He believed Douglas had played a key role in allowing slavery to spread. Lincoln decided to run against him for his seat in the U.S. Senate.

PREPARING TO MEET

In June 1858, Illinois Republicans chose Lincoln as their candidate for the U.S. Senate race. He believed slavery was wrong, but he knew the U.S. Constitution had no laws that made the practice illegal. Still, he did not think the founders of the United States would have wanted slavery to spread into new territories and states. Lincoln's views upset some Illinois voters. Abolitionists, who wanted slavery to end right away, were discouraged that Lincoln did not want to make slavery illegal for all states. In addition, Lincoln angered Illinois voters who backed popular sovereignty or disliked African-Americans.

Douglas was once again the Democrats' candidate for the Senate. But he had lost the support of those who wanted to end the spread of slavery when he wrote the Kansas-Nebraska Act. Still, Douglas had the support of people in Illinois who liked popular sovereignty or disliked blacks.

In July, Douglas spoke in Chicago. The next night,

Lincoln spoke in the same hall and attacked Douglas' views on slavery. For the next several weeks, Lincoln followed his opponent across the state. Wherever Douglas spoke, Lincoln spoke within days. A newspaper that supported Douglas called Lincoln a "poor desperate creature" because "the people won't turn out to hear him."

Lincoln decided to challenge Douglas to a series of face-to-face debates. Douglas did not want to debate him.

Douglas' and Lincoln's July speeches were given at the Tremont House hotel in Chicago.

The Lincoln-Douglas debates took place across the state throughout the late summer and fall.

Lincoln would gain attention from the press, and Douglas risked blurting out something that would offend voters. But Douglas did not want voters to think he was afraid of Lincoln, so he finally agreed to seven debates. The first

27

debate was scheduled for August 21 in Ottawa, a town in northern Illinois that strongly supported the Republicans. Other debates would take place in towns with mostly Democratic voters who supported slavery.

Thousands of people were expected to attend each debate. Americans in 1858 did not have many choices for entertainment. Radio, television, recorded music, and movies had not been invented. Going to political speeches

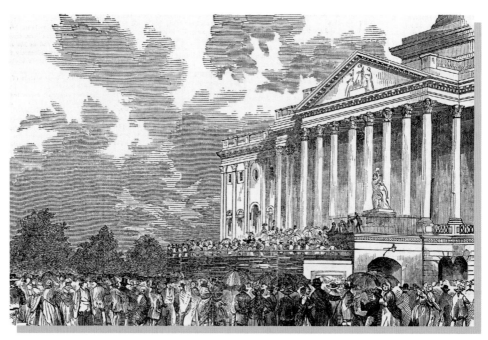

As a popular outing, political speeches like this one in the 1850s drew large crowds.

and debates was a popular way to spend free time.

The people of Illinois were eager to hear Lincoln and Douglas. Both men were known as excellent public speakers. Douglas had a deep voice, and he laid out his arguments carefully. At times, he read from notes that he brought with him onstage. Lincoln's voice was higher, and a friend of his once said it could be "shrill ... and squeaky." As he spoke, however, Lincoln's voice lowered and became more pleasant. Lincoln sometimes told jokes and stories as he spoke, which his audiences enjoyed.

THE DEBATES BEGIN

On Saturday, August 21, 1858, as many as 15,000 people filled the public square in Ottawa, Illinois. Lincoln later said there were "more [people] than could [get] close enough to hear." Lincoln and many of his supporters had

Lincoln was a foot taller than Douglas.

come to Ottawa by train. A parade with brass bands and soldiers marched with Lincoln as he walked to the mayor's house. He waited there until it was time for the debate to start. Douglas also made a grand entrance into town. He rode in a carriage pulled by six white horses.

Douglas started the debate with an hour-long speech. He argued that Lincoln and other Republicans were really abolitionists, despite what they said. Douglas often referred to them as "black Republicans," and suggested

A political cartoon features Douglas as a gladiator. He was a fierce debater.

they wanted to help blacks gain more rights and equal treatment. Douglas knew that many people in Illinois had racist views—even if they opposed the spread of slavery.

31

Few people were willing to admit that blacks and whites were equal and should have the same rights. Douglas made clear where he stood. He agreed with the Dred Scott decision that blacks should never be citizens. Douglas added, "I do not believe that the Almighty [God] ever intended the negro to be the equal of the white man."

Douglas also questioned a comment Lincoln had made in an earlier speech. The Republican had said that the United States could not survive unless slavery was either allowed or outlawed throughout the country. Douglas argued that the United States had survived for 70 years with both slave and free states, and it could continue that way. Throughout his speech, Douglas challenged Lincoln to say exactly what he thought about the issues relating to slavery.

Lincoln then took the podium for a 90-minute response. He began by saying once again that slavery should not be allowed in territories where it did not already exist. But he promised, "I have no purpose directly or indirectly to interfere with … slavery where it already exists."

Lincoln also said that he agreed with Douglas that blacks and whites were not the same in every way. But he believed that every man was equal in the way spelled out in the Declaration of Independence. That document from 1776

The Declaration of Independence states the basic rights for U.S. citizens.

had created the United States by joining the 13 British colonies into one independent nation. The Declaration said all men had the right to "life, liberty, and the pursuit of happiness." Blacks, Lincoln said, deserved those rights.

Lincoln responds to Douglas' speech at the first debate in Ottawa.

A slave was denied his liberty and the right to "eat the bread … which his own hand earns."

Throughout the speeches, members of the audience cheered and clapped for the candidate they liked, and teased and taunted his opponent. At one point, Douglas spoke harshly against Lincoln. One of the senator's supporters yelled for Douglas to "hit him again." When Lincoln asked the crowd, "What is popular sovereignty?" some of his supporters shouted, "A humbug."

After the debate, the Republican newspaper from Chicago said Lincoln was "powerful," while Douglas was "cowardly." Another reporter noted that "the town is alive with excitement; bonfires are blazing on every corner, and magnificent torch light procession, accompanied by two bands of music, is parading the streets, and everywhere the cry is 'Hurrah for Lincoln!'"

Meanwhile, Chicago's Democratic newspaper reported that Douglas "electrified the crowd." It said Lincoln avoided Douglas' tough questions and looked uncomfortable. Some of Lincoln's supporters seemed to agree. One man wanted Lincoln to attack Douglas with stronger words: "Let us see blood every time [Lincoln] closes a sentence." But Douglas saw that Lincoln was a strong debater. Douglas admitted that Lincoln was "the most difficult and dangerous opponent that I have ever met."

In the second debate at Freeport, Lincoln seemed more forceful than in his first speech. He responded to comments Douglas had made in Ottawa. Lincoln said

Douglas and other Democratic leaders wanted to nationalize slavery, or make it legal throughout the country. The Kansas-Nebraska Act and the Dred Scott decision were part of that effort. Douglas, however, denied that there was a secret effort to nationalize slavery. This issue came up again in later debates.

The debates continued into October. At each spot, Douglas tried to show that Lincoln said one thing in one place and something different in another. In particular, Douglas claimed that Lincoln denied he favored equal rights for blacks when he spoke in southern Illinois—the most racist part of the state. But Lincoln argued he did not change his message to suit the audience. He always said that blacks deserved the rights that are spelled out in the Declaration.

However, Lincoln did make some comments that seemed designed to win support from racists. In Charleston, Illinois, he said, "There is a physical difference between the white and black races which I believe will for-

The fifth Lincoln-Douglas debate took place on the Knox College campus in Galesburg, Illinois.

ever forbid the two races living together on terms of social and political equality." Nevertheless, in the last debate in Alton, Lincoln made it clear that he thought slavery was wrong. Douglas, meanwhile, emphasized that his main concern was popular sovereignty. "I care more for the … right of the people to rule than I do for all the negroes."

37

AFTER THE DEBATES

Many U.S. newspapers closely followed the Lincoln-Douglas debates. Americans knew the two candidates were discussing something that affected the whole country. Some Americans thought that one of the two men would run for U.S. president in 1860.

By the last debate, the crowds were not as large. Newspapers had published the earlier debates, so people knew what each candidate would say. Douglas and Lincoln made many of the same points over and over. After Alton, Douglas and Lincoln continued to give speeches separately. Then they waited until it was time for the Illinois Legislature to decide who would be the state's senator.

Douglas, who had already been a presidential candidate in 1856, wanted to hold on to his seat in the Senate. In that position, he would remain an important Democratic leader and have a chance to win the presidency in 1860. Lincoln also seemed to build support for a

38

future presidential election. He was not yet known nationally, but his speeches had drawn some attention. He was becoming a powerful spokesman for the new Republican Party.

plause.]

I have stated upon former occasions, and I may as well state again, what I understand to be the real issue in this controversy between Judge Douglas and myself. On the point of my wanting to make war between the free and the slave States, there has been no issue between us. So, too, when he assumes that I am in favor of introducing a perfect social and political equality between the white and black races. These are false issues, upon which Judge Douglas has tried to force the controversy. There is no foundation in truth for the charge that I maintain either of these propositions. The real issue in this controversy — the one pressing upon every mind—is the sentiment on the part of one class that looks upon the institution of slavery *as a wrong*, and of another class that *does not* look upon it as a wrong. The sentiment that contemplates the institution of slavery in this country as a wrong is the sentiment of the Republican party. It is the sentiment around which all their actions—all their arguments circle—from which all their propositions radiate. They look upon it as being a moral, social and political wrong; and while they contemplate it as such, they nevertheless have due regard for its actual existence among us, and the difficulties of getting rid of it in any satisfactory way and to all the constitutional obligations thrown about it. Yet having a due regard for these, they desire a policy in regard to it that looks to its not creating any more danger. They insist that it should as far as may be, *be treated* as a wrong, and one of the methods of treating it as a wrong is to *make provision that it shall grow no larger*. [Loud applause.] They also desire a policy that looks to a peaceful end of slavery at sometime, as being

Lincoln kept a scrapbook of the Illinois campaign. It included items like this speech excerpt.

After the fall election, there were more Democrats than Republicans in the Illinois Legislature. The Democratic vote helped Douglas beat Lincoln 54-46. When he learned he had won, Douglas said, "Let the voice of the people rule." Lincoln wrote to a friend, "The cause of … liberty must not be surrendered at the end of *one,* or even, one *hundred* defeats."

No one can say for sure if the debates helped Douglas beat Lincoln. Republican candidates actually won more votes in the counties where the two men held their debates. But the debates helped Lincoln in 1860. That year, he published a book with newspaper reports of the debates. The book became popular across the United States, and it helped voters get to know more about Lincoln and his ideas.

That June, the Republicans chose Lincoln to be their candidate for U.S. president. Douglas, meanwhile, was the choice of Northern Democrats. The Southern Democrats split from Northern Democrats and ran a third candidate, John C. Breckinridge. A fourth candidate, John Bell, was nominated by the Constitutional Union party.

A political cartoon shows Uncle Sam telling presidential candidates John Bell, John C. Breckinridge, and Stephen Douglas that Lincoln already has the job.

Lincoln won the election, which led to the secession of several Southern states. After the Union split, Douglas and Lincoln met to discuss the state of the nation. The men agreed that the Southern states had to be brought back into the Union. Douglas told Lincoln he needed "to save our children a country to live in." Douglas died in June 1861, just after the Civil War began. Lincoln was able to save the Union as Douglas had wanted. The president also achieved another important goal: ending slavery in the United States.

Lincoln helped keep the Union together.

41

GLOSSARY

abolitionists—people who fought to end slavery

economy—the way a country runs its industry, trade, or finance

humbug—something intended to deceive or mislead

latitude—imaginary lines that measure distances north or south of the equator

militia—troops made up of local residents who volunteer during a crisis

racist—judging people based on race or skin color

repealed—officially canceled an existing law

seceded—broke away from a country

territories— areas of land belonging to the United States that are not states

DID YOU KNOW?

- During the 1858 campaign, Stephen Douglas gave a total of 130 speeches, while Lincoln gave 63. The two men traveled by boat, train, and horse-drawn carriage to meet with voters.

- The debate at Galesburg was thought to have drawn the largest crowd, with about 20,000 people attending. The Jonesboro debate had the smallest crowd—around 2,000 people.

- By the last debate in Alton, Douglas was losing his voice, and part of his speech could barely be heard by the audience.

- In the presidential campaign of 1860, Lincoln won the vote in 17 states, all in the North. Douglas won only the state of Missouri. Two other candidates, John Bell and John Breckinridge, won the other slave states. Lincoln and Douglas split the vote in New Jersey.

43

IMPORTANT DATES

Timeline

1830	Abraham Lincoln moves to Illinois.
1833	Stephen Douglas moves to Illinois.
1836	Douglas and Lincoln serve together in the Illinois Legislature.
1842	Douglas is elected to the U.S. House of Representatives.
1847	Lincoln begins term in the U.S. House of Representatives; Douglas is elected to the U.S. Senate.
1854	Douglas writes the Kansas-Nebraska Act.
1858	Lincoln and Douglas hold their seven debates across Illinois; Douglas defeats Lincoln for the U.S. Senate.
1860	Northern Democrats choose Douglas as their candidate for president; Republicans choose Lincoln, who wins the election.
1861	The Civil War begins.

IMPORTANT PEOPLE

JOHN BELL (1796–1869)

U.S. congressman from Tennessee who was the Constitutional Union party's candidate for president in 1860

JOHN C. BRECKINRIDGE (1821–1875)

U.S. congressman from Kentucky who was the Southern Democrats' candidate for president in 1860

STEPHEN DOUGLAS (1813–1861)

Popular senator from Illinois who was known for his strong speaking skills; he was the Northern Democrats' candidate for president in 1860

ABRAHAM LINCOLN (1809–1865)

Illinois politician who gained national fame during the 1858 U.S. Senate race in Illinois; he was elected the 16th president of the United States in 1860 on the Republican ticket

LYMAN TRUMBULL (1813–1896)

Political leader who strongly opposed slavery; he won a seat in the U.S. Senate in 1854 after Abraham Lincoln dropped out of the race

WANT TO KNOW MORE?

At the Library

Anderson, Dale. *The Causes of the Civil War.* Milwaukee, Wis.: World
  Almanac Library, 2004.

Bonner, Mike. *Stephen A. Douglas: Champion of the Union.* Philadelphia:
  Chelsea House Publishers, 2002.

Isaacs, Sally Senzell. *America in the Time of Abraham Lincoln: 1815 to 1869.*
  Des Plaines, Ill.: Heinemann Library, 2000.

Roberts, Jeremy. *Abraham Lincoln.* Minneapolis: Lerner Publications, 2004.

Rossi, Ann M. *Freedom Struggle: The Anti-slavery Movement, 1830-1865.*
  Washington, D.C.: National Geographic, 2005.

On the Web

For more information on the *Lincoln-Douglas Debates*, use FactHound
to track down Web sites related to this book.

1. Go to *www.facthound.com*

2. Type in a search word related to this book
   or this book ID: 0756516323

3. Click on the *Fetch It* button.

Your trusty FactHound will fetch the best Web sites for you!

On the Road

Douglas Monument Park
636 E. 35th St.
Chicago, IL 60616
312/225-2620
A statue of Stephen Douglas
marks where he is buried

Abraham Lincoln Presidential Library & Museum
112 N. Sixth St.
Springfield, IL 62701
217/558-8844
A research library and museum
dedicated to the life of Abraham
Lincoln; includes display on the
Lincoln-Douglas Debates

Look for more We the People books about this era:

The Assassination of Abraham Lincoln
ISBN 0-7565-0678-6

The Battle of Gettysburg
ISBN 0-7565-0098-2

Battle of the Ironclads
ISBN 0-7565-1628-5

The Carpetbaggers
ISBN 0-7565-0834-7

The Emancipation Proclamation
ISBN 0-7565-0209-8

Fort Sumter
ISBN 0-7565-1629-3

The Gettysburg Address
ISBN 0-7565-1271-9

Great Women of the Civil War
ISBN 0-7565-0839-8

The Missouri Compromise
ISBN 0-7565-1634-X

The Reconstruction Amendments
ISBN 0-7565-1636-6

Surrender at Appomattox
ISBN 0-7565-1626-9

The Underground Railroad
ISBN 0-7565-0102-4

A complete list of We the People titles is available on our Web site:
www.compasspointbooks.com

INDEX

About the Author

Michael Burgan is a freelance writer for children and adults. A history graduate of the University of Connecticut, he has written more than 90 fiction and nonfiction children's books for various publishers. For adult audiences, he has written news articles, essays, and plays. Michael Burgan is a recipient of an Educational Press Association of America award.